The Winter of Love

By Jim Wortham

Jim Wortham

James Wortham Publishing Company
P O Box 40
Madison, Indiana 47250-0040 U.S.A.

Email: JimWortham123@gmail.com

Autographed books may be ordered
direct from author.
See page 133 for order information.

The Winter of Love

Art via Unsplash, Pixabay
Editor & Typesetter: Gypsy Mercer
Book & Cover Design: Gypsy Mercer

Excerpts by permission of author and publisher:
  Be Gentle With Your Goodbye/Jim Wortham
  Notes On How To Hang In There/Jim Wortham

*Author's note: this is a work of fiction. Names, characters,
places and incidents are a product of the author's
imagination. Any resemblance to actual people, living or
dead, or actual events is purely coincidental.*

The Winter of Love/Jim Wortham ~ First Edition
ISBN 978-1928877226

Library of Congress Control Number: 2020918967

<u>Dedication</u>

To you

Allow me to wipe away your sadness

Let me touch your loneliness

We have traveled down the same road

We made it this far

We are almost there

Have faith

Jim Wortham

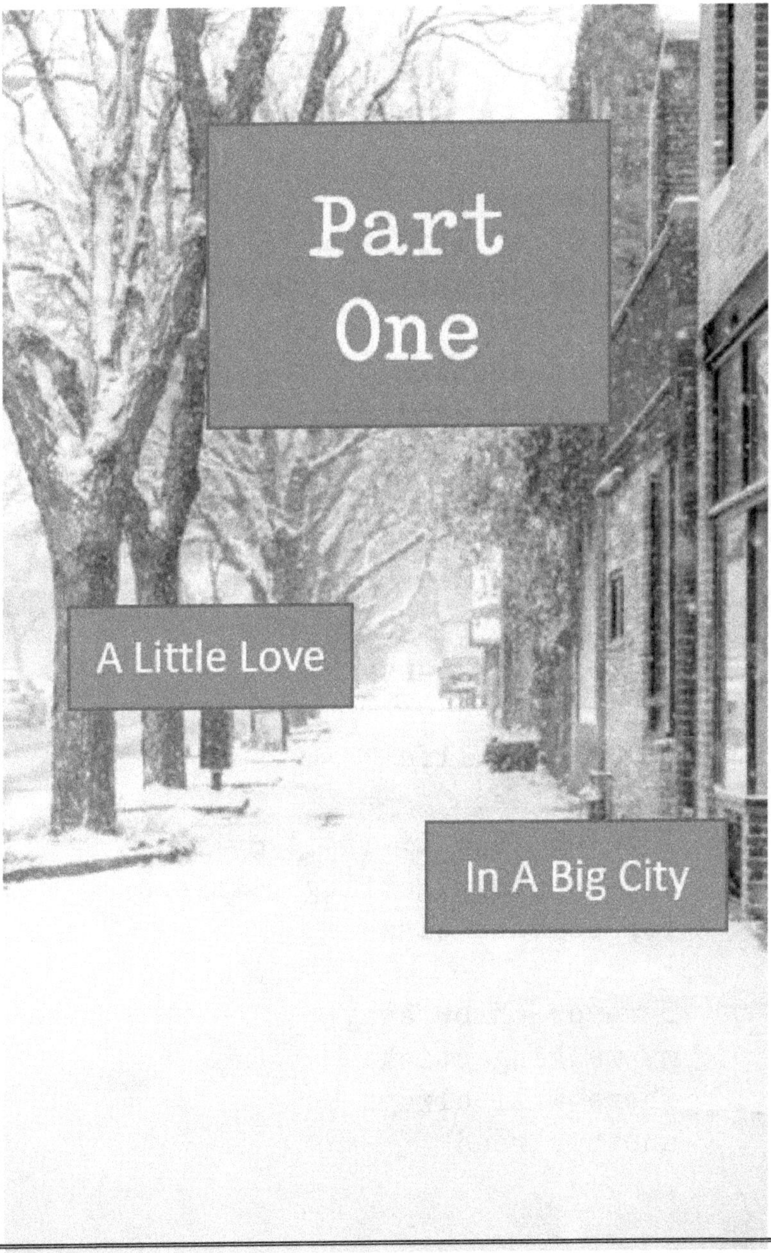
Part
One
A Little Love
In A Big City

Jim Wortham

Pieces of Love

I have spent
most of my life
walking unfamiliar streets

Once in a while
a friendly wanderer
crosses my path
We celebrate finding each other
and for a brief time
I become aware
of what love can do
    to my hopes
    to my days
    to my life
Then it ends
I never know if it is my fault
or the other getting restless
for someone else

I never throw away
my walking stick
There will always be
another road

Bye Lady

It has been months
I have tried to forget
   your walking away
      your final goodbye

These last few days
I have walked
crowded city streets
but never once
did I look for you
or see your face within my mind

I even
crossed the streets
without reaching out
for your hand

I did not miss you

I am content
and happy now
I am ready
to begin again

Jim Wortham

My Love

You cannot
leave me
to chase your dream

then ask
to return

One goodbye is
more than enough

Winter

Our two months
seeing each other
every day
was perfect love

until you
discovered
I was
imperfect

Jim Wortham

Talking It Out

Talking

about it

helped

smooth

our differences

Mention Me

Tomorrow
you may
mention me once
then
forget my name

I could love you
I could love you a lot

I could be so happy
with you

Love causes one
to be foolish
to say foolish things
It is much too soon
to say this

I should not tell you
Forgive me

Jim Wortham

Don't

You say
you want me
because I
reach for dreams

You have seen me
with only a smile
and poetic lips

If you could
see me now
        f
        a
        l
        l
        i
        n
        g
to my knees
with broken dreams
in hand
you would turn
and walk away

Getting High

You call it a natural high
breathing in sunshine
on the beach
listening to waves splashing
taking the bad
making it good
searching for beauty
in everything

Jim Wortham

She Cries

A teenage girl
had
many
expensive things

But there was
no one
to love her
as she grew up

Alone

The songwriter

sits on the

apartment floor

writing

on scraps of paper

hoping

tomorrow

will bring

love

Jim Wortham

Singer

He sits
strumming a guitar
singing his songs

He has a box nearby
with kittens in it
Children play with them

A crowd stops
listens
pitches dimes and dollars
into the box
with the kittens

He lives this way
hoping he will be discovered

He is a Greenwich Village
street singer
living on a dream

His Room

A warped guitar
two broken strings
propped up against
the wall
of his room

Desk still cluttered
with magazines
books
records

The picture of his girl
still hangs above the bed

Nothing has been changed
or touched

His voice echoes
to all who enter the room
who knew him

The dusty floor
still collects tear drops
each time the door opens and closes

Once Upon A Yesterday

Our story could have been
we lived happily ever after

but you would not give
us a chance
you wanted to fall in love
with everyone you met

Now later in life
your hair graying
you ask me to return
to the relationship
we once had

I am sorry
You are too late

Reflections of Mildred's Pond

The pond looked the same tonight
as I sat down beside it
The grass is a little higher
the crickets make their
old familiar sounds
I saw a crescent moon
like the one we used to see

I sat there thinking
it was only days ago
then realized
it has been many years since then

I glanced into the pond
something had changed
through the years
No longer were there reflections
of a couple kissing
only the images
of a lonely old man

Laugh

If there be
no wedding song for us
then during these moments

take my hand

walk with me

laugh with me

cry with me

If there be
no wedding march for us
I still want
these memories

Precious Moments

When we

get together

I wish

time

was

a

broken

watch

Footsteps

I only wanted
to be your friend
to listen to
your experiences

Your sharing
was honest
even your faults

I never meant
to love you
but
my heart
began to listen
for your steps

Caring

Pain
came to the 80-year old
mother

as she waved
goodbye
to her only son

Once the mother
cared for someone

Now there is no one
to care
for her

Jim Wortham

Reno

The clouds cried
the day you moved to Reno
You had time to write stories
to touch trees
to ride in a canoe

In Reno
your job rushes you
far into the night
Your eyes have become
dark and hollow
Your speech is harsh

Here
time is still slow
Your almost finished novels
are still waiting
There is even enough time
to hear voices
calling you home

City Streets

I walk the streets
ugly
to one who cannot find work
Even prison seems safer
more secure

The wealthy
rush
to catch heart attacks

I look into an old woman's face
I see pain
from broken love
distasteful jobs

The bum seems happiest
He asks for quarters
He slows time
savoring each moment
He tastes the streets
leaving all else behind

Jim Wortham

I Should Have Listened

How was I to know
one day
I would call
but you would no longer answer
?
You were always there
How was I to know that our time
was about to end
?
If I could do it over
I would take time to talk each day
I would withhold unkind words

I was self-centered
missing times
we should have enjoyed

How I miss you

I will
always
miss you

Smell the Coffee

It is becoming more difficult
making it through the day
alone

If the day gets too tough
if my mind seems to
sing the blues too loudly
I will make a list
of three things to do
and expect no more from myself

I never cared for coffee
when I was younger
I only drank it to socialize

A friend called asking me to
meet for coffee
We agreed on a coffee shop

I am going to meet my friend now
I feel better already
This will be the third
and final thing
on my list
to do today

Jim Wortham

Broken Wings

No poems
No songs
No music
There are no creative juices
anymore

There must be a disconnect
from the creative flow
that streams from
reading
hearing
playing other people's
poems
songs
music

It is time to plug into
the streaming creative flow
again
and
again

Part Two

Hang

In

There

Jim Wortham

Thank you for dropping by
Do not give up your dreams
I put mine in the attic
They are still there
My dream was to be a poet
living off my poetry
I did for a while
It has been years
Here is the good news
I am picking up my pen
beginning again
Hang in there with me
I have lots to share

There are many
ups
and
downs
during this ride

I
only
have to
hold on
long
enough

Jim Wortham

Looking around
I notice
most people
do not use
their ability
to do the things
in life
they want to do

It does not take
much talent
nor
much ability

The trip requires
a little of
one
or
the other
or a combination
of both

The rest of the trip
to the dream
is a road
paved with determination

Jim Wortham

I have listened
too often
to losers

They tell me
I cannot do
the
thing
I want to do

Why do I listen
to everyone
who says
I cannot do it
?

Most of all
why do I believe them
?

I should listen
to people
who are
going places

Who do not know
or will not acknowledge
the word
impossible

They turn the world
upside down
if they need to
to get
where they are going

Jim Wortham

It is like this

>   Yesterday
>   I met a beautiful lady
>   eighteen years old
>   She had won awards
>   in college plays

>   I found her in
>   a rustproofing office
>   giving estimates
>   I asked her
>   why this job
>   ?

She said
everyone convinced me
that after high school
I should get a job
make a living
So I did

I really wanted to be an actress

I could not make her
change her mind
She would not let go
of her job
to follow her dream

I was sad
because
I knew
she could have made it

The trip
would not
have been long

Jim Wortham

I sit down
over hot tea
and ask myself
what if Sylvester Stallone
had been worried about
finding a secure job
instead of writing
Rocky
?

After all
Sylvester
did you not know that
a married man
earning thirty or forty
dollars a week
is not enough
for the average man
?

What kept you going
?

The problem is
I listen
to the wrong people

They cannot help me
They only
poison
my mind
with their doubts

Jim Wortham

I have allowed
other people
to feed
fears
into me

just like a
computer programmer
inputs data into a computer

A computer cannot erase
its own tapes

I can
erase
my negative tapes
I can
feed my mind
with positive vibrations
doing the very thing
my inner voice
tells me
I should be doing

Jim Wortham

Security
is not
the answer

Security breeds sameness
sameness breeds dullness
dullness drains creative energy
and
the dream
never
gets reached

I look
within
myself
to find security

No longer
will I hold
on to things
or
situations
sabotaging
my thoughts

Jim Wortham

My dream

is happening now

if I let go

of doubt

and ride with the flow

When

I relax

and let it happen

I move

in the right direction

I am not afraid

Fear

is leaving

Fear

waves its arms

at me

Fear of the unknown

Fear of letting go of things I know well

Fear of failing

Fear of losing things

Fear of failing

Always that fear of failing

Jim Wortham

I get a glimpse
of what it will be like
if my dream comes true

The music
on the other side
is lovely

In order to be

happy

I have to have

a freer

flow of energy

Tensions

leave

as I flow

Jim Wortham

The problem with letting go
and flowing with the energy
is the fear of
not knowing
what will happen

Even if I do not
let go
I still do not know
what will happen

My friend Joe
had a secure job
but was replaced
with a machine
the other day

The future
cannot be known
My mind must
realize that

Other people

put a price

on an hour

of my time

My time

cannot be

related to money

It is the only

life I have

It is worth whatever

I want to believe it is

Jim Wortham

I am told to rush
get the job done
not to waste time

I am tired
of the big rush
Maybe
I would like to linger
or waste time
Maybe
that is worth
a million dollars
to me

I like Ted
Ted quit his job
at the machine factory
when he was fifty

He started a bookkeeping service
in his home
went door-to-door
to find customers
Kinfolk thought he was crazy
to leave the security of
his machine job

Now Ted has a big home
cars
leisure time for trips
flowing energy
Ted is happier than
a teenage girl
getting ready for a date

Jim Wortham

Change

is a constant

in living

I do not try

to stop it

Change flows

I must

flow

I will not do
what I do not
need to do

I often stay
busy
I only miss
spontaneous happenings
which are the things
that mean the most
to me

Jim Wortham

I have to push
fear
out of my mind
when I first detect it

If I do not
fear
will multiply
and overcome me

With the first sight of
fear
I stamp it out
I get rid of it

I refuse
to grab
skeletons
from the closet
of yesterday

I refuse
to imagine
disaster in the future
Fear of the future
is a trick

The future
does not exist
I am no longer tricked
into believing it does

Jim Wortham

Today is good
Tomorrow
will be good

Maybe better

I flow
with the days
as they flow

I get high

on non-drugs

like

Becoming aware

Aware of the taste of food

Aware of the sounds outside my window

Of the touch of another hand on mine

Of cooking hamburgers on a grill

Jim Wortham

I am

where I am

because of the amount

of confidence

I have in myself

I have unborn dreams

because of my lack of confidence

Yes

my world is what it is

because of the

dreams

I dared to believe in

My dreams

have materialized

in direct proportion

to my self confidence

Jim Wortham

I created

where I am now

I create

now

what and where

I want to be

Now

all my dreams

will come true

Life

is changing

Change

must happen

I let my change be for good

I let my change be

in the direction

of where I wish to go

Jim Wortham

I drop

everything

that I am doing

that I do not need

I drop

everything

but the essentials

Less weight

around me

is what I want

Now I can move faster

I keep

my mind

still

I pick up

the direction

I should go

Jim Wortham

Nothing
is more important
than doing
what is right for me

It is almost
too simple
to believe
that I should be
what I want to be

and only
what I want to be

Many people

ignore what they want to do

in order to please others

They end up doing

what other people

want them to do

I cannot waste time anymore

I will not waste time

How much time is left

?

Jim Wortham

Time

is ticking

away my life

It keeps getting

less

for each of us

Think about it

Why
should I
waste my life
living out other people's
unfulfilled dreams
?

After all
they
had their chance

Now
it is
my time
to
become

Jim Wortham

When
I feel uneasy
about a decision
I am about to make
I do nothing

Anything
that feels wrong
is wrong

Anything
that feels right
is right

Do not fight
what is right

Do it

Do not fight
what is wrong

Do not do it
Stop

I do not make decisions
when I am depressed
A negative mind breeds
wrong choices
I wait for a change
in my attitude

I make decisions
when I am
on top of things
when my thoughts are high

If help

never comes my way

I pick myself up

brush myself off

give myself a pep talk

and move on

Jim Wortham

It has taken

a long time

to come to this realization

but it had to be this way

It was worth

the wait

for the illumination to come

I catch a glimpse
over the walls
of what security is

A new life
is on the other side

I will claw
or climb
if I must
but I will get over

I will be at home
for the first time
on the other side

We are all artists

only different kinds

We must expand our talents

for others

to enjoy

With each passing day
the voice of fear
becomes weaker

In the background
fear calls out to me
saying I will fail
I should seek material security

I let fear's voice
fade with the sounds
of cars passing
Each passing day
I become more confident in myself
and my dream becomes closer

Jim Wortham

I am letting go
of everything
pulling me away
from my dream

It has taken
a long
long time
to come to this point

I am starting to feel
good
about this

New confidence
has arisen
from within

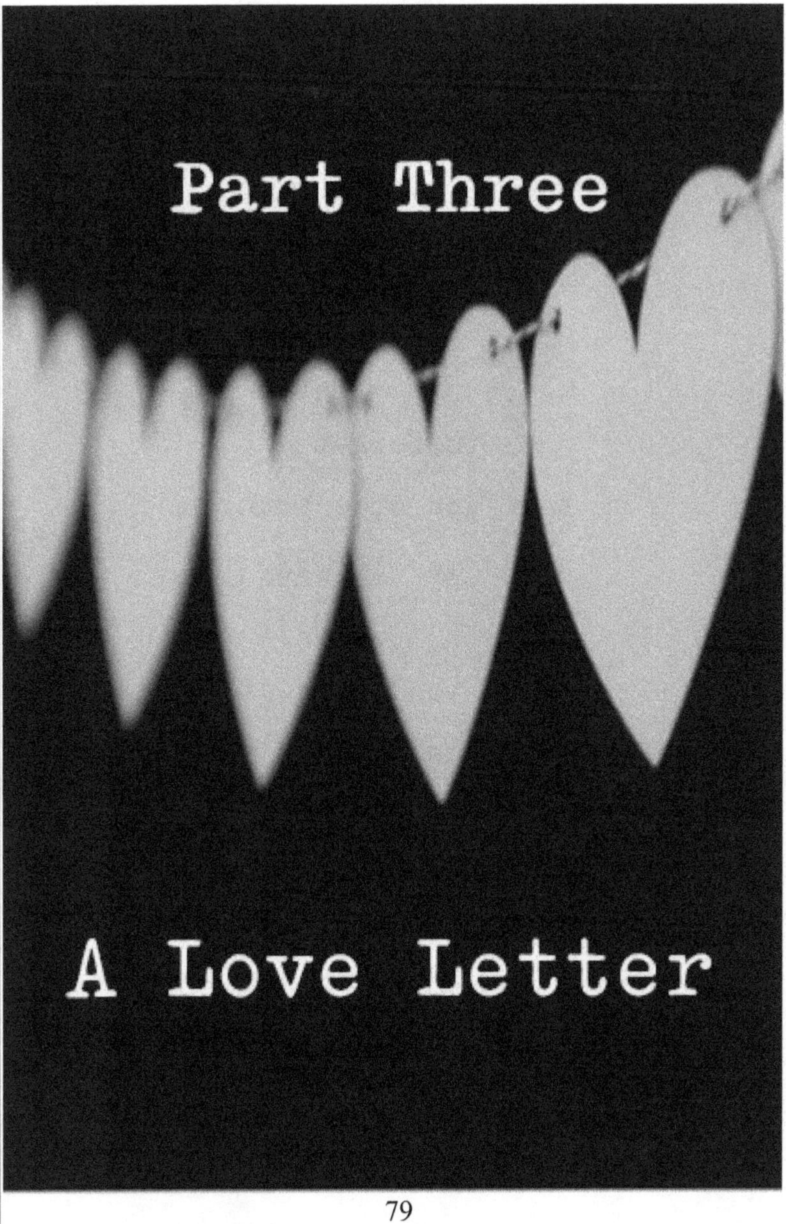
Part Three
A Love Letter

Jim Wortham

It seems as if
15 years would be
long enough
for me
to forget
the face of a young
and lovely lady

I am wondering if
15 more years
or even 50
will erase
your face
from the theater
of my mind

I stop time

tonight

to send

mental messages

to you saying

Hello

wherever

you

are

!

Jim Wortham

I guess you look different now
Time will not stop for anyone
not even your beauty

If your years have been like mine
you have been hurt
many times
by uncaring lovers
Many dreams lay abandoned
within the broken pages
of your soul

I cannot imagine anything bad
happening to you
I can only see a young girl
with flirting eyes
laughter
reaching for life

My mind will not let you
grow old

I am older
People call me a mature man
with responsibilities
holding down a good job

No one would ever imagine
there is a young boy of 18
hidden within my mind
who fell so much in love
with you

It is as if that 18-year old boy
has stayed with me
never aged a day
since the day
our paths
took different directions

Jim Wortham

At night

the little boy

unpacks

snapshot

memories of you

telling him

his love has bouncy hair

dancing & enchanting eyes

a soft and kind voice

She is alive and will come back

some day

And the boy

is convincing

with his hypnotic voice

Your sensitivity

was unmatched

when I told a lie

just to impress you

You would know

You always knew

You would seem embarrassed

for me

look toward the sky

or glance down

You never said anything

You did not have to

Jim Wortham

In my mind
I see our last date
I remember distinctly
how you had fallen in love
with someone else
That night
you told me
you cared for me
but
you could never feel love for me
like you felt for
that
other
person

I never wanted to see
that
other
person
for fear of what
the hate in me
might do

That final date

without a goodbye kiss

caused the boy in me

to close the door

and

stop life at 18

searching every moment

for a glimpse

of your return

Jim Wortham

I always hoped
we would
in some mysterious way
find a pathway
back to each other
like in fairy tales

That boy in me
has been
listening
for
your footsteps

What makes living difficult

is not knowing

where you are now

You might be here

in my town

working

as an elementary school teacher

or

running

an advertising agency

I might be walking

past your office

each day

without knowing it

Jim Wortham

Sometimes
I think I see you
crossing the street
When I almost catch up
you step into a bus
or walk into a department store

Once I called out your name
You stopped
as if you recognized my voice
Our eyes did not meet
and you disappeared

Each time
I barely miss you
it hurts

My throat tightens
tears clog my throat
my chest pounds wildly

I almost
reach you every time
but not quite

Jim Wortham

When I feel as I do
the boy in me
causes me to hope

I want to get up
run out of my house
and look for you in
discos
malls
concert halls
everywhere
until our eyes
embrace
once again

What if I did find you
tonight
Would your hair have the same
softness
?
Would your voice carry the same
warmth
?
Would you still reach
with laughing eyes
to touch my hand
?
My face
?

Jim Wortham

If we ever meet
face to face
will our honesty still be there
?
Or will past experiences
with unfaithful lovers
cause us to be afraid
?

Can we remove our masks
?
Will the sensitivity
shine through
?

Will I hear
My friend
it is so good to see you
I hope we meet again
Must go now
Bye

If we ever meet
but could not continue
where we left off 15 years ago
I think the man that I am
would stop living
The cause
slow death
due to
neglect

Because of this
I am torn between
not wanting to see you again
and
searching a lifetime for you

Jim Wortham

If and when

we ever meet

and

the magic

causes love to bind us

the little boy inside me

will become the man

I am meant to be

and

I will be

complete

Part Four

Notes

From

Leonard's Cafe

Jim Wortham

I must not

waste time

on nonessentials

Life is too short

Activities

Schedules

Deadlines

have robbed me

of spontaneous experiences

I hear

Slow Down!

Slow Down!

Time is my gift

Whether I succeed

or fail

the outcome

leans on

what I do

now

If I had listened more

to my inner voice

I might be nearer

to where I am going

Jim Wortham

Sitting at a table
sipping hot chocolate
watching a candle talk
I tell it how
someday it will be

I think of how
it will be better
tomorrow
next month
next year

I make plans
to change my situation

I am

responsible

for what I am

All good

all bad

are the result

of my actions

I control

what is happening

in my little world

even if it turns

without me

Jim Wortham

I can change
where
I am

I need only analyze
what I do
to get where
I want to be

I can
change tomorrow
today

I think of how
I used to be shy
I overcame it
I made myself talk to strangers
until fear ran

At times
I am still shy
I force myself
to talk

even to
myself

Jim Wortham

I admire Roy
because he makes time
to barbecue ribs
to take trips

I wish I would make time

Living high
is not necessary for me
My car eats my living
I could be just as happy
with a junker
But I will not
let go

I do not
want to remain
where I am

I have energy in me
to
make my dreams real

Too long
I have allowed
"I cannot do it" thoughts
to dominate me

I rebel
I am ready to fight
for my dreams

Jim Wortham

I must remember
to be logical
realistic

How can I accomplish
what I want
?
How have others
accomplished it
?
If they did it
I can too

There are many ways
of getting there
I must discover
one

I eat alone in this dim café
A big turkey sandwich
tastes good
with plenty of Tiger Sauce

I am away from it all
I have time to talk
to my hot chocolate

I ask myself questions
Is my job really that bad
                ?
            Well
I want a different one

Is my situation doable
                ?
            Well
if I can change it
I will find a way

Jim Wortham

I allow my mind

to roam

It goes in

exciting directions

I push away worry

and let my mind

entertain

me

My mind sends messages to Judie
1000 miles away

Do you ever take time
to remember that Christmas
                  ?

We ate at McDonald's
drove back to your place
Our spirits touched

We could be happy
if distance had not
broken our connection

Tonight
over hot chocolate
with one marshmallow floating
I think of you
and smile

Jim Wortham

Some girls are eyeing me
from another table

My mind returns
to where I am
I see a bulb
flickering out

The juke-box forces
more experiences
to jump from yesterday
A cold football game
comes to mind

A nickel in the juke-box
makes yesterday come back

It is time to move on

The marshmallow

has melted in the chocolate

and a white topping

is floating

It is cool outside

I breathe deeply

Tomorrow is coming

Jim Wortham

My life
Your life

each a
masterpiece

is happening
now

Part Five

God
will
you
be
my
Friend
?

Jim Wortham

Colors

I made a mistake
by chasing dreams

I should have
smelled the flowers
watched the sky change colors

I should have slowed down
to feel the touch of God
to share a prayer
    with a crying girl
and to touch another's hand

As I look at the calendar
of time
I see it is not too late
to begin
today

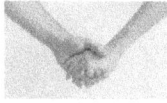

Dead End

Mike once knew God
He has been running
and doing his own thing
so long
that he thinks he is happy

He has a scared look
on his face
each time he talks
with a Christian
who reminds him of the peace
he once had

Jim Wortham

A Tiny Glimpse

You sat in the choir
singing and radiating
a mystical smile

Your smile blinded me
kept me from seeing others
sitting around you
You were happy
I wanted to know you

I made plans in my mind
I saw us being together
exploring secrets from the
Book of God
        like two children
        digging
        through a toy chest

Gap

I search my thoughts
trace each thought
I unlock each secret compartment
inside my mind

I must find
my secret sins, Jesus,
so I can get rid of them
You see
I want to be friends
with you again
I am just not getting through
There seems to be a
communication gap

Jim Wortham

What Flavor Ice Cream?

Sometimes I wonder
If you were living in the flesh today
what would you do after High School
                    ?
Would you drive the newest sports car
or be satisfied with a junker
                    ?
What kind of music would you listen
to
                    ?
What do you like on your hamburger
                    ?
Cheese?   Mustard?   Ketchup?
Onion?

Would you visit Baskin Robbins
            Ice Cream Shop
                    ?
What flavor ice cream would you
choose
                    ?

It Is Over

Tonight ended it
She walked away from me
to someone new

I must accept
that I am not who she needed
My throat tightens
I want to be alone
letting the tears flow
                      flow
                           flow
Jesus, help me realize
it is best for the breakup
to happen now
not later

Assure me
there will be someone special
I will love more
and make the waiting easy
Please

Jim Wortham

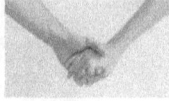

Touch Life

You are young
trying to reach out
telling everyone
about your experiences
with Jesus

I see some people rejecting you
Others are accepting your words
Their lives are being changed

Keep smiling
Keep reaching
You can change the world

Easy Talk

He tells me
a drink of liquor
helps him talk better, Jesus
He calls it a social stimulant

He tells me
if he is with a pretty lady
he can loosen up
and talk easier about things

He wants to know
how liquor can be bad
if he drinks moderately

Give me the right words
to tell him

Jim Wortham

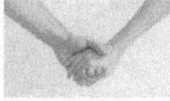

Out of Touch

Today he
        looks
        for something real
        to believe in

Today he
        looks
        for a way out
        of his meaningless
            existence

Today he
        looks
        for someone
        to show love towards him

Meanwhile
            today's Christians
            hope and pray
            to be used by God

Meanwhile
            today's Christians
            remain quiet
            so they will not offend
            anyone

Meanwhile
            the searching individual
            falls deeper into
            this meaningless world

Jim Wortham

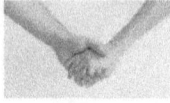

Getting High

Judie gets so

                          h

                     g

                 i

              h

on God's love

She never sinks

                  d

                    o

                      w

                         n

to loneliness

Prayers & Promises

Walking along the beach

you and I

stop

to offer

silent prayers

giving thanks

for having met

Jim Wortham

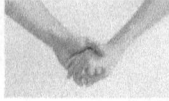

Lonely

Jesus, do you see my friend
?

She is thirty-three
divorced
has a son eight years old

She says no man will get
involved with her
It would mean too much responsibility

Who will care for her, Lord
?

Bring someone her way
who really cares

I Had No Words

He came to me for a word of hope
He is not smiling
not himself
Sleep is rare and disturbed
He is not able to eat
He picks at the food on his plate
He cannot go on much longer

I call on additional help
Lord
hear his inner cries
give him hope
direct him to right choices

Jim Wortham

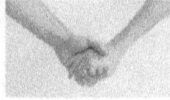

Solid Rock

You are always there
Always, God

Bad things have come my way
like when I spent a summer
selling books to earn enough
money to go to college
and came home broke

More recently
I took a job which is very
difficult

Sometimes I wonder why I
get trapped into all these things

Is it my fault

?

Or is this the path I must follow
to get to where I need to be

?

I do not know
But you are always there
to see me through to the next place
Always, God

Jim Wortham

The World Spins Too Fast

The world spins too fast
for gentle people

My closest friends
ran the race
We were going to have it all
We became tired
and did not keep in step

Where was the race to end up
?
Was there a pot of gold
or promise of health
or forever friends
?

It has been awhile
a long while
since I started the race
I have slowed down

I sleep late now
Not up before ten
or later
if the doorbell does not ring

Where are all the runners
in a race we started
                ?

The world spins too fast

Jim Wortham

Where Are The Gentle People?

Where have the gentle people gone
?

There were not many
but I did meet a few

I am thinking of a friend who would
fight me to pay the lunch bill

I am thinking of the couple
who gave me their place
in line because my arms
were full

I do not want those who deceive me
to be my friends

I want the gentle people to return
to my life

The Seasons of Love Series

The Summer of Love $ 9.95

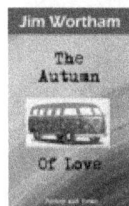

The Autumn of Love $ 9.95

The Winter of Love $ 9.95

The Spring of Love $ 9.95

Thank you for reading my book.
Autographed copies are available from
Jim Wortham, PO Box 40
Madison, Indiana 47250-0040 U.S.A.
Email: Jim Wortham123@gmail.com

Shipping within the United States is
$5 for the entire order. Contact me
for overseas shipping costs.

Jim Wortham

Follow Jim Wortham

Jim's blog: www.JimWorthamPoet.com
Facebook: www.facebook.com/Jim.Wortham.54
Jim's email: jimwortham123@gmail.com

Jim Wortham Poetry Books
Post Office Box 40
Madison, Indiana 47250-0040
U.S.A.

Autographed books available